Tutti-Fruity

"A Baby is
for a short period of time
In your arms,
but for a lifetime
In your heart.

This is worth more
than silver or gold,
A feeling money
can not buy
and a memory
no one can steal"

*May this book
bring your joy
- Colette*

**Please like our face book page
Colette Art Therapy**

*This book can also be personalised
with photos of family and friends.
See our website for more information.*

www.ColetteArtTherapy.com

Copyright © 2020. Published by **Treasure_my_Art**

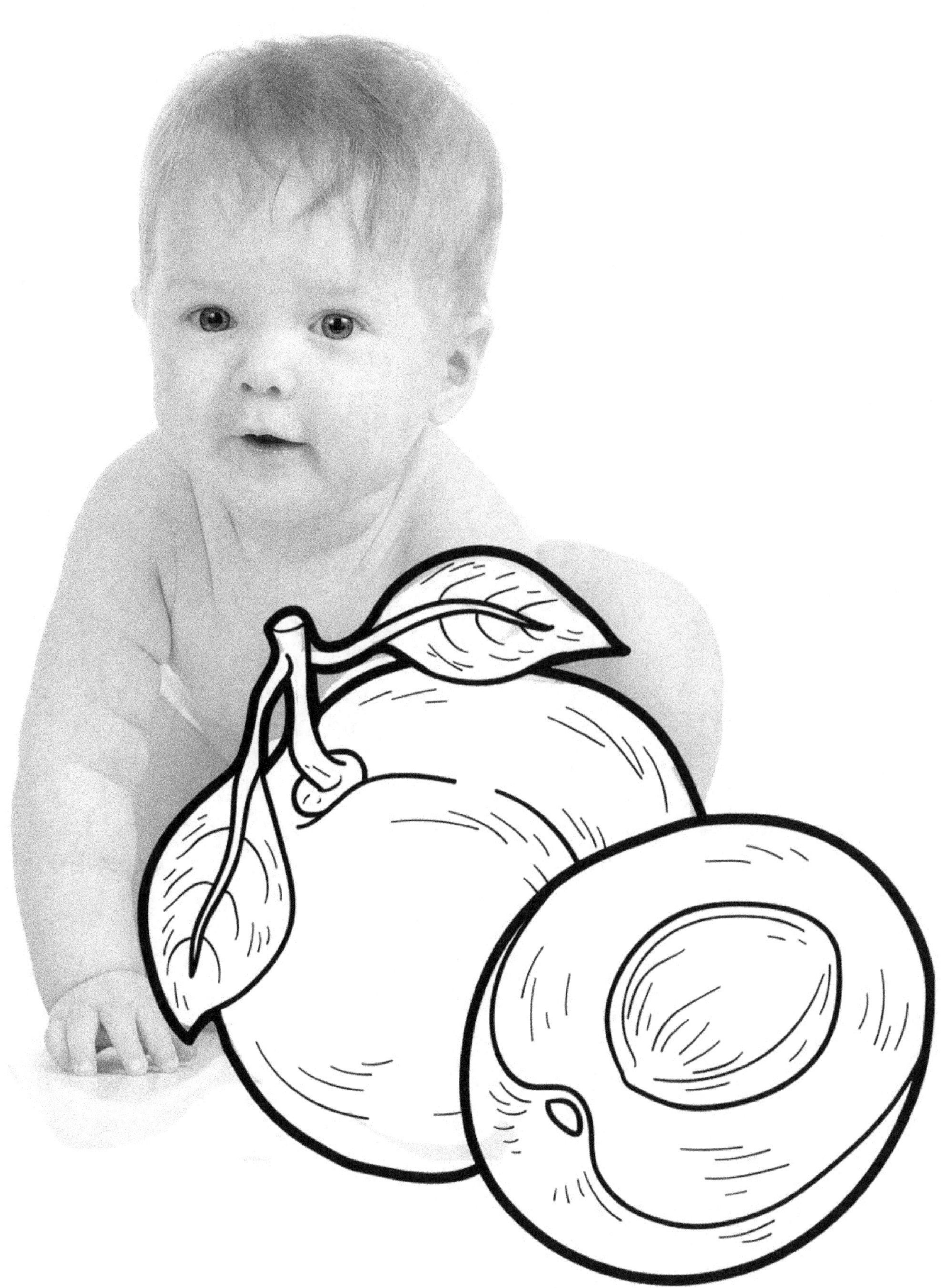

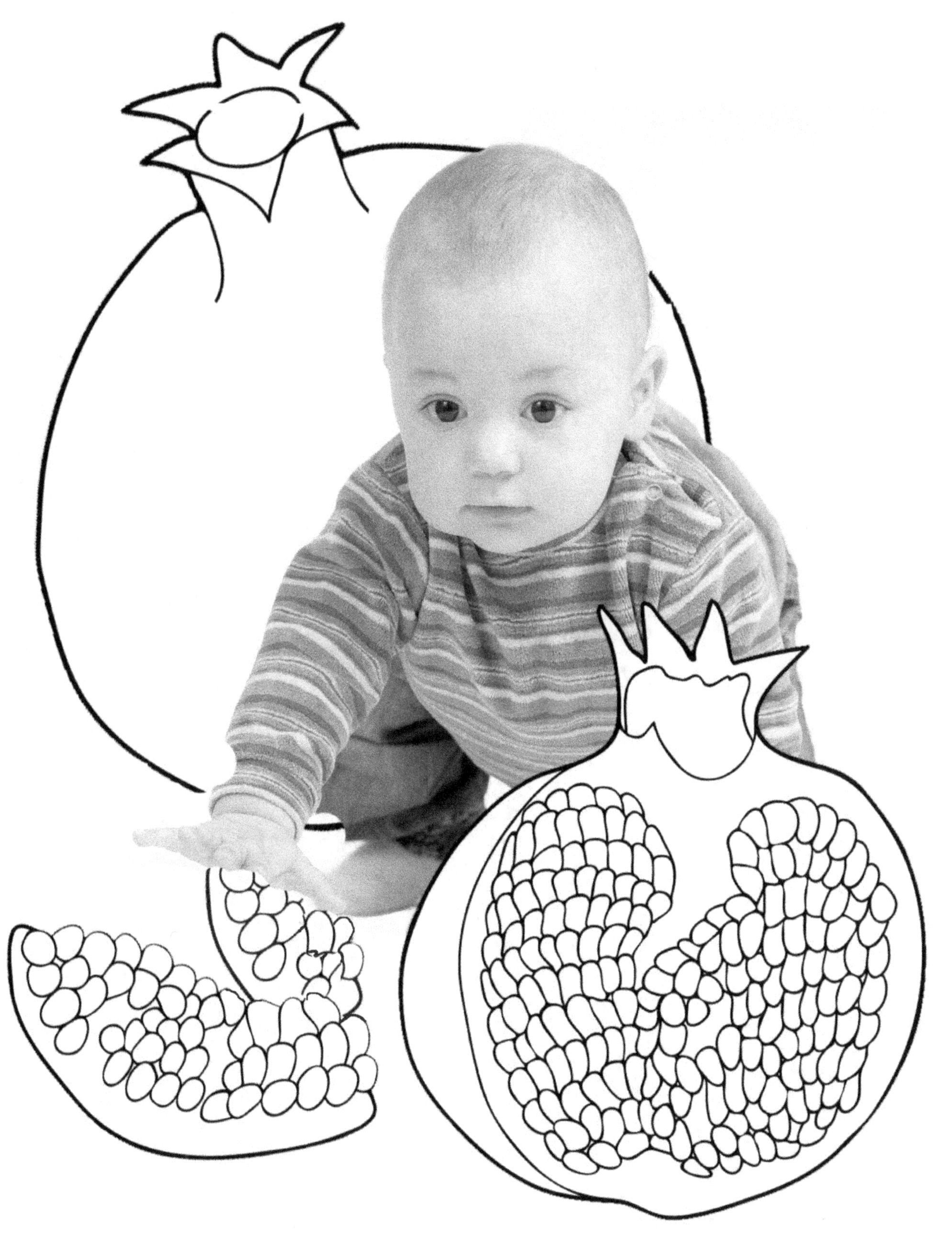

Also available in this Babies for Dementia Range

The Ocean   Babies and Flowers   Cupcakes   Butterflies

A Picture from our book
Babies and the Ocean

Please like and share our Face Book page

Colette Art Therapy

Www.ColetteArtTherapy.com